CW00945628

THE WISDOM OF
THE ANGLO-SAXONS

THE WISDOM
OF THE
ANGLO-SAXONS

Compiled by Gordon Mursell

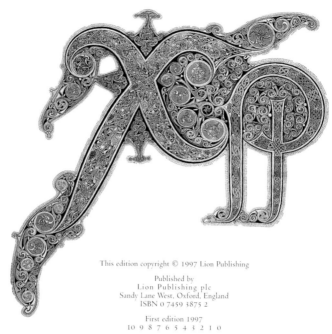

This edition copyright © 1997 Lion Publishing

Published by
Lion Publishing plc
Sandy Lane West, Oxford, England
ISBN 0 7459 3875 2

First edition 1997
10 9 8 7 6 5 4 3 2 1 0

A catalogue record for this book is available
from the British Library

Printed and bound in Singapore

Series editor: Philip Law
Project editor: Angela Handley
Book designer: Nicholas Rous
Jacket designer: Gerald Rogers

Contents

Introduction

Christianity came to England from two
directions – from the British and Irish kingdoms
of the west and north which had embraced the
new religion during the fourth and fifth
centuries; and from the south, in the person of
the Roman missionary Augustine of Canterbury.
During the seventh century these two different
traditions – the Irish Celtic, and the Roman –
met in Northumbria, where the primacy of the
latter was effectively established at Whitby in
664. But the Anglo-Saxon population of England
did not overnight abandon its pagan beliefs and
customs: the names still given to the days of the
week derive from the old Germanic pantheon,
and testify to the enduring nature of some at
least of these beliefs and customs; and the new
religion triumphed over the old by
christianizing it, rather than by destroying it.

The wisdom of the Anglo-Saxons is thus a rich mixture of pagan and Christian; and it reflects the character of an unsettled, often violent, age. Christ is a heroic figure, triumphing over the cosmic powers of evil on the cross; and the saints are presented as both attractive and powerful,

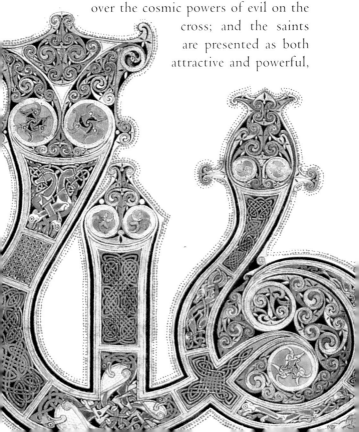

exuding an authority that even the animals recognize and obey. Above all, life was a journey through an often wild and startling landscape; and prayer was supremely a plea for protection, companionship and healing in a hazardous and often hostile environment.

A profound sense of wonder marks Anglo-Saxon thought: people loved heroic sagas, richly carved crosses, gorgeous jewellery, all of them sources of light and strength in the midst of danger. The best was both in the past and in the future, only fleetingly in the present: this world was a land of exile, and the highest and holiest wisdom was that which enabled you to pass safely through it to the great halls of paradise, where pagan heroes and Christian saints waited to bid you welcome.

GORDON MURSELL

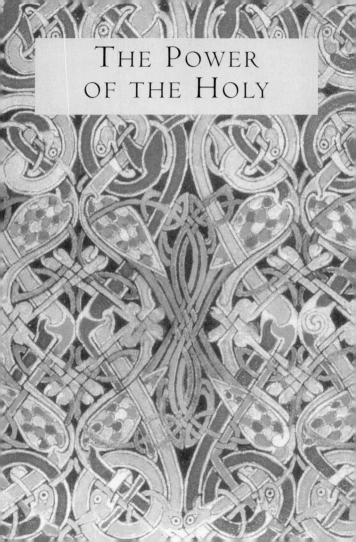

THE POWER
OF THE HOLY

THE DREAM OF THE TREE AT CALVARY

Then the young hero (who was God Almighty)
Got ready, resolute and strong in heart.
He climbed onto the lofty gallows-tree,
Bold in the sight of many watching men,
When He intended to redeem mankind.
I trembled as the warrior embraced me.
But still I dared not bend down to the earth,
Fall to the ground. Upright I had to stand.
A rood I was raised up; and I held high
The noble King, the Lord of heaven above…
I saw the God of hosts stretched grimly out.
Darkness covered the Ruler's corpse with clouds,
His shining beauty; shadows passed across,
Black in the darkness. All creation wept…

The Dream of the Rood

St Cuthbert and the Otters

Cuthbert was in the habit of rising at the dead of night, while everyone else was sleeping, to go out and pray, returning just in time for morning prayers. One night one of the monks watched him creep out, then followed him stealthily to see where he was going and what he was about. Down he went towards the beach beneath the monastery and out into the sea until he was up to his arms and neck in deep water. The splash of the waves accompanied his vigil throughout the dark hours of the night. At daybreak he came out, knelt down on the sand, and prayed. Then two otters bounded out of the water, stretched themselves out before him, warmed his feet with their breath, and tried to dry him on their fur. They finished, received his blessing, and slipped back to their watery home.

Bede's Life of St Cuthbert

3

THE POWER OF THE CROSS

If someone recites seven prayers to the cross in one day, or venerates a cross seven times, the seven doors of hell will be closed to him and the seven doors of paradise will be opened to him. If your first duty is to the cross, even if all the demons should be around you, they will not be able to harm you. Whoever does not bow to the cross does not receive for himself the Passion of Christ; the one who bows receives it and is freed. And whatever land you give to the cross, it is as if you offer to the Lord that much from your own inheritance.

From a late Anglo-Saxon manuscript

PRAYER FOR SPIRITUAL HEALTH

O Lord Jesus Christ, who gave power to your
apostles to heal the sick, raise the dead, cleanse
lepers, and cast out demons, give me true humility,
a firm faith, patience in my tribulations, and
health of mind and body; and establish in
my heart holy thoughts: direct my feet in the
way of peace that I may hold fast to justice in my
manner of life, discipline in my actions, and in
all things that fear of you which is the beginning
of wisdom. O reconciler of the human race,
I beseech you on account of your name and
through the prayers of your apostles, to hear me,
God and Holy One of Israel, and mortify the evils
of all my vices through the multitude of your
mercies; restore me both inwardly and outwardly
with your gifts, and enlighten the darkness of my
heart by the light of your unending love.

From an Anglo-Saxon Prayer Book

THE HEALING POWER OF NATURE

This herb, which men call betony [bishopwort],
grows in meadows, and in clean downlands and
in protected places. It [is good] either for a
man's soul or his body; it shields him against
dreadful nightgoers and against fearful visions
and dreams. This herb is very holy, and thus
you should gather it.

The Anglo-Saxon Herbal

THE SPIRITUAL
JOURNEY

THE SEAFARER

I sing my own true story, tell my travels,
How I have often suffered times of hardship
In days of toil, and have experienced
Bitter anxiety, my troubled home
On many a ship has been the heaving waves,
Where grim night-watch has often been my lot
At the ship's prow as it beat past the cliffs.
Oppressed by cold my feet were bound by frost
In icy bonds, while worries simmered hot
About my heart, and hunger from within
Tore the sea-worthy spirit. He knows not,
Who lives most easily on land, how I
Have spent my winter on the ice-cold sea,
Wretched and anxious, in the paths of exile,
Lacking dear friends, hung round by icicles,
While hail flew past in showers. There heard
   I nothing
But the resounding sea, the ice-cold waves...

Night shadows darkened, snow came from the
   north,
Frost bound the earth and hail fell on the
   ground...
And yet the heart's desires
Incite me now that I myself should go
On towering seas, among the salt waves' play;
And constantly the heartfelt wishes urge
The spirit to venture, that I should go forth
To see the lands of strangers far away.

The Seafarer

THE DIVINE NAVIGATOR

Then Wisdom said: 'Through goodness God created all things, because He Himself rules everything which we said was good; and He alone is the steady ruler and steersman and rudder and helm, because He guides and governs all creation just as a good steersman guides a ship.'

King Alfred the Great

THE SWAN

My dress is silent when I tread the ground
Or stay at home or stir upon the waters.
Sometimes my trappings and the lofty air
Raise me above the dwelling-place of men,
And then the power of clouds carries me far
Above the people; and my ornaments
Loudly resound, send forth a melody
And clearly sing, when I am not in touch
With earth or water, but a flying spirit.

Riddle from The Exeter Book

GOD THE ANCHORHOLD

Look directly with your mind's eye at God, just as directly as the ship's anchor-cable is stretched in a straight line from the ship to the anchor; and fix your mind's eye on God as the anchor is fixed in the ground. Even though the ship is on the waves out at sea, it is safe and sound if the cable holds, because one of its ends is fixed in the ground and the other is fixed to the ship.

King Alfred the Great

THE HEAVENLY COUNTRY

For a good person the day he dies is happier than the day he is born, for it is the start of peace, as the latter is of pain. We are born to die; we die to live better. This life is a road to our own country.

A Letter of Alcuin (732–804) to Charlemagne

WISDOM FOR THE JOURNEY

Give rein to your natural gifts and abilities; do
not stifle your literary talents and your keen
spiritual understanding with gross pleasures
of the flesh... Put aside all harmful obstacles;
strive with unflagging zest to pursue your
study of the scriptures and thereby acquire
that nobility of mind which is divine wisdom...
[which will] guide you to the shore of an
enchanting paradise and the everlasting bliss
of the angels.

Letter of St Boniface (680–754) to Nithard

BEDE'S DEATH SONG

Before the journey that awaits us all,
No man becomes so wise that he has not
Need to think out, before his going hence,
What judgment will be given to his soul
After his death, of evil or of good.

Letter of St Cuthbert concerning the death of Bede

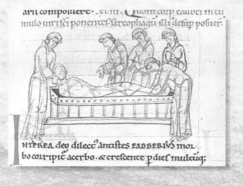

THE WISDOM OF PARADISE

'All is hardship
On earth, the immutable decree of fate
Alters the world which lies beneath the heavens.
Here property and friendship pass away,
Here man himself and kinsmen pass away,
And all this earthly structure comes to nought.'
Thus spoke the thoughtful sage, he sat apart.
Blessed is he who keeps his faith; a man
Must never be too eager to reveal
His cares, unless he knows already how
To bring about a cure by his own zeal.
Well shall it be for him who looks for grace
And comfort from our father in the heavens,
Where is ordained all our security.

The Wanderer

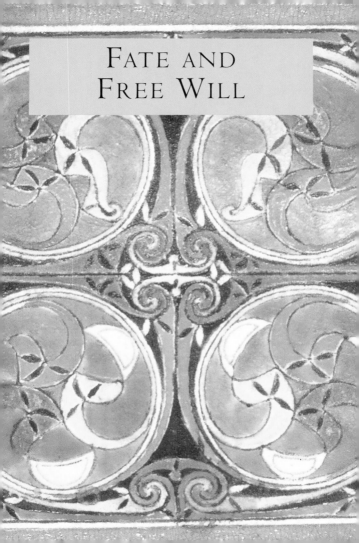

FATE AND
FREE WILL

THE LAWS OF NATURE

Grief is remarkably hard to shake off. The clouds roll on... A hawk must go on a glove, the wild thing stay there. The wolf must be in the forest, wretched and solitary, the boar in the wood with his strong, fixed tusks. A good man must gain honour in his own country. The javelin goes in the hand, the spear that glitters with gold. On a ring a jewel should stand large and prominent. A river must mix in the waves with the sea's current. A ship must have a mast, a standing spar for sails. The splendid iron sword must lie in the lap. A dragon must live in a barrow, old and proud of his treasures. A fish must spawn its kind in the water. In the hall a king must share out rings. A bear must live on the heath, old and terrifying. A river must run downhill in a grey torrent...

God's place is in heaven, he is the judge of deeds. A hall must have a door, the building's broad mouth. A shield must have a boss, a firm finger-guard. A bird must play, up in the air. In a deep pool the salmon must glide with the trout. Stirred by the wind the shower shall come down to this world from the sky.

Poems of Wisdom and Learning in Old English

THE FLIGHT OF THE SPARROW

When we compare the present life of man with that time of which we have no knowledge, then it seems to me like the swift flight of a lone sparrow through the banqueting-hall where you sit in the winter months to dine with your thanes and counsellors. Inside there is a comforting fire to warm the room; outside, the wintry storms of snow and rain are raging. This sparrow flies swiftly in through one door of the hall, and out through another. While he is inside, he is safe from the winter storms; but after a few moments of comfort, he vanishes from sight into the darkness whence he came. Similarly, man appears on earth for a little while, but we know nothing of what went before this life, and what follows. Therefore if this new teaching can reveal any more certain knowledge, it seems only right that we should follow it.

From Bede's History of the English Church and People

FATE AND FREE WILL

Fate is hard to alter, it surges up very often;
it causes tears, it piles up sorrows, it injures
the spirit, it carries the years along. And
nevertheless one who is intelligent can
moderate all the things that fate causes, as
long as he is clear in his mind and is prepared
to seek help from his friends, and moreover
enjoy the Holy Spirit.

Poems of Wisdom and Learning in Old English

SEEKING WISDOM FOR THE END
OF ALL THINGS

A man should wait, before he makes a vow,
Until in pride he truly can assess
How, when a crisis comes, he will re-act.
The wise must know how awesome it will be
When all the wealth of earth stands desolate,
As now in various parts throughout the world
Stand wind-blown walls, frost-covered, ruined
   buildings.
The wine-halls crumble; monarchs lifeless lie…

The Wanderer

TRUE PRAYER

PRAYER FOR THE MORNING

May we walk in prosperity in this day of light:
In the power of the most high God, greatest
   of the gods,
In a manner pleasing to Christ,
In the light of the Holy Spirit,
In the faith of the patriarchs,
In the merits of the prophets,
In the peace of the apostles,
In the joy of the angels,
In the splendour of the saints…
In abundance of peace,
In praise of the Trinity,
With our senses alert,
With constant good works,
With the spiritual powers,
With a holy life,

In these things is the journey of all labouring
    for Christ who leads his saints after death
    into eternal joy
That I may hear the voice of the angels
    praising God and saying Holy, Holy, Holy.

The Book of Cerne (c. 800)

PRAYER AND ACTION

Prayer as a whole is not only in the words by
which we invoke the divine mercy, but also in
all the things which we do in the service of
our Maker by the devotion of faith... For
how could anyone invoke the Lord with words
in every hour and moment without a break?
But we pray without ceasing when we perform
only those works which commend us by our
godliness to our maker.

Bede's Commentary on the Gospel of St Mark

PRAYER FOR PROTECTION

I ask you O Lord to send your delight into my
heart and your love into my senses, and to let
your mercy cover me.

The Book of Cerne

KING ALFRED'S PRAYER

Lord God Almighty, maker and ruler of all creatures, I beseech You on behalf of Your mighty mercy, and through the sign of the Holy Cross, and through St Mary's maidenhood, and through St Michael's obedience, and through the love and merits of all Your saints, that You guide me better than I have done towards You; and direct me according to Your will and my soul's need better than I myself am able, and protect me from my enemies visible and invisible; and teach me to perform Your will, that I may inwardly love You before all things with pure thought and clean body, for You are my Creator and my Redeemer, my sustenance, my consolation, my trust and my hope.

King Alfred the Great

PRAYER TO THE WOUNDED CHRIST

O wonderful dispenser of the divine medicine, who allowed your side to be opened with the spear, open to me knocking, I beg, the door of life and, having entered through it, I will acknowledge you; through the wound in your side, cure the wounds of all my sins through the medicine of your mercy, lest I should ever be made guilty of your body and blood by receiving it unworthily, as a punishment for what my sins deserve; but grant that my soul may be filled with the abundance of your mercies and that you who are my ransom may also be my reward, O Lord Jesus Christ.

The Book of Nunnaminster (c. 800)

PRAYER FOR THE NATION

Lord, have mercy
Christ, have mercy
O Christ, hear us.
Saint Michael, pray for us.
Saint Gabriel, pray for us.
Saint Raphael, pray for us.
All the holy angels, pray for us.
Saint Peter, pray for us.
Saint Paul, pray for us.
All the holy choir of apostles, pray for us.
Saint Samson, pray for us.
Saint Gildas, pray for us.
Saint German, pray for us.
Saint Columba, pray for us.
All the holy choir of confessors, pray for us.

We sinners beseech you to hear us:
that you may grant us life and health, and
    perseverance in good works,
that you may deign to keep us in true faith and
    religion,
that you may grant us the fruits of the earth,
    serenity of sky, and rain in due season,
that you may deign to protect the English clergy
    and people, and the whole company of the
    faithful,
Christ, have mercy,
Lord, have mercy,
Christ, have mercy.

Tenth-century Breton Prayer for the English Nation

THE PRAYER OF THE RAVENS

One day some ravens which had long inhabited the island of Lindisfarne were seen tearing the straw from the roof of the visitors' house and carrying it off to build their nests. The saint reproved them: 'In the Name of Jesus Christ, depart forthwith!' he shouted. They flew off shamefacedly almost before he had finished speaking. Three days later one of a pair of them returned, and finding Cuthbert digging, stood before him, with feathers outspread and head bowed low to its feet in sign of grief. Using whatever signs it could to express contrition it very humbly asked pardon.

When Cuthbert realized what it meant, he gave permission for them all to return. Back they came with a fitting gift – a lump of pig's lard. 'What care should not men take,' Cuthbert would say, 'to cultivate obedience and humility when the very birds hasten to wash away their faults of pride by prayers, tears, and gifts?'

Bede's Life of St Cuthbert

PRAYER OF A HOLY WOMAN

The holy Margaret looked to the heavens and said, 'Strengthen me, Spirit of life, so that my prayer may travel through the heavens and may ascend before your sight. And send me your Holy Spirit from the heavens, which may come to my aid, so that I may preserve my virginity undefiled and that I may see my enemy, who fights against me, face to face, and so that I may ever be an example and an inspiration to all women who believe in you, for your name is blessed in eternity.'

Old English Life of St Margaret

A PRAYER OF LONGING

O Lord Jesus Christ, who crossed from this world to the Father, and loved those who were in the world, make my mind cross from earthly to heavenly things; make it despise all that is falling away and desire only heavenly things, and make me long to burn with the fire of your love. And you, O God, who condescended to wash with sacred hands the feet of your holy apostles, purify my heart by pouring upon it the light of the Holy Spirit, that in all things and above all things I may be able to love you, our Lord Jesus Christ. Amen.

From an Anglo-Saxon Prayer Book

CARE FOR THE POOR

We are all God's poor; let us therefore
acknowledge the poor who ask of us, that
God may acknowledge us, when we ask our
needs of him. Who are those that ask of us?
Those who are poor, and feeble, and mortal.
Of whom ask they? Of those who are poor,
and feeble, and mortal. Except the possessions,
alike are those who ask and those of whom
they ask. How canst thou for shame ask
anything of God, if thou refuse to thy fellow
that which thou canst most easily grant him?

Sermon of St Ælfric (955–1020)

PRAYER FOR A SICK ANIMAL

May the beasts on earth be healed, they are vexed in health; in the name of God the Father and the Son and the Holy Spirit let the Devil be expelled through the imposition of our hands; who shall separate us from the love of Christ; through the invocation of all your saints; through Him who lives and reigns forever. Amen. Repeat 'Lord, wherefore they are increased' [Psalm 2] thrice.

Prayer for use when a horse is afflicted

PRAYER FOR GOD'S GRACE

And do thou, great Father of lights, from whom every good gift and every perfect gift cometh down, Who hast given to me, the humblest of thy servants, both love for the wonderful things of thy law and aid in meditating upon them, and who, in the treasury of the prophets, has furnished me with the grace, not only to embrace things old, but also in very truth to find new things under the veil of the old and to bring them forth for the use of my fellow-servants, remember me, O my God, for good.

Bede's Commentary on Ezra and Nehemiah

THE VICTORY OF GOD

May God be friend to me,
He who once suffered on the gallows tree
On earth here for men's sins. Us He redeemed
And granted us our life and heavenly home.
Hope was renewed with glory and with bliss
For those who suffered burning fires in hell.
The Son was mighty on that expedition,
Successful and victorious; and when
The one Almighty Ruler brought with Him
A multitude of spirits to God's kingdom,
To bliss among the angels and the souls
Of all who dwelt already in the heavens
In glory, then Almighty God had come,
The Ruler entered into His own land.

The Wanderer

Text Acknowledgments

Extracts 1 ('The Dream of the Rood', c. 750), 6 ('The Seafarer', lines 1–38 passim), 8 (Riddle 7 in the 'Exeter Book'), 12 ('Bede's Death Song', from 'The Letter of Cuthbert concerning the death of Bede,'), and 13, 17 and 30 ('The Wanderer'), trans. R. Hamer, *A Choice of Anglo-Saxon Verse*, Faber, 1970, pp. 97, 127, 181–83, 187–89, 97. Extracts 2 and 24: Bede, 'The Life of St Cuthbert', chap. 10, trans. J.F. Webb, in *The Age of Bede*, Penguin Classics, rev. ed. 1988, pp. 55–6. Extract 3: From a late Anglo-Saxon manuscript, British Library Cotton Titus D.xxvii, 70r-v, quoted and translated in Barbara Raw, *Anglo-Saxon Crucifixion Iconography*, Cambridge University Press, 1990, p. 64. Extracts 4 and 26: From *A Pre-Conquest English Prayer-Book*, ed. B.J. Muir, Henry Bradshaw Society, 1988, pp. 48–51 and 54, translated by the compiler. Extracts 5 ('The Anglo-Saxon Herbal') and 28 (A prayer for use when a horse is shot, i.e. afflicted by an ailment believed to have been the result of an elf attack): trans. O. Cockayne, cited in K.L. Jolly, *Popular Religion in Late Saxon England*, North Carolina University Press, 1996, pp. 135, 143–44. Extract 7: Bede, Homily 2:8, Latin original in 'Opera homiletica', ed. by D. Hurst, *Corpus Christianorum*, Latin Series vol. 122; Turnhout, Belgium, 1982, translated by the compiler. Extract 9: Alfred the Great, additions to his translation of St Augustine's 'Soliloquies', ed. & trans. by S. Keynes and M. Lapidge, in *Alfred the Great*, Penguin Classics, 1983, p. 140. Extract 10: Alcuin (732–804), Letter to Charlemagne on the death of his friend, English translation by Stephen Allott in *Alcuin of York*, William Sessions, 1974, p. 107. Extract 11: St Boniface (680–754), Letter to Nithard, English translation by C.H. Talbot, *The Letters of Saint Boniface*, Columbia University Press, 1940, p. 66. Extracts 14 and 16: From *Poems of Wisdom and Learning in Old English*, English translation by Tom Shippey, D.S. Brewer, 1976, pp. 77, 99. Extract 15: From Bede *A History of the English Church and People*, translated Leo Sherley-Price, Harmondsworth, Penguin rev. ed. 1965, pp. 124–25. Extracts 18 and 20: From 'The Book of Cerne' (c. 800), in *The Prayer Book to Aethelwald the Bishop, commonly called the Book of Cerne*, ed. Dom A.B. Kuypers, Cambridge, 1902, pp. 91–92 and 141, translated by the compiler. Extract 19: Bede, 'Commentary on the Gospel of St Mark (In Marci evangelium expositio)' III, translated by the compiler. Extract 21: Alfred the Great's additions to his translation of the 'Consolation of Philosophy' by Boethius, 34:11, ed. & trans. by S. Keynes and M. Lapidge, in *Alfred the Great*, Penguin Classics, 1983, p. 134. Extract 22: From 'The Book of Nunnaminster' (c. 800) translated by Barbara Raw in *Anglo-Saxon Crucifixion Iconography*, Cambridge University Press 1990, p. 125. Extract 23: From a tenth-century Breton prayer for the English nation; original in *Anglo-Saxon Litanies of the Saints*, ed. M. Lapidge, London: Henry Bradshaw Society, 1991, pp. 259–64, translated by the compiler. Extract 25: From 'The Old English Life of St Margaret', ed. & trans. by M. Clayton and H. Magennis, Cambridge University Press, 1994, p. 119. Extract 27: Ælfric, Sermon on the Greater Litany, in *The Catholic Homilies*, ed. Thorpe, trans. slightly altered, The Ælfric Society, 1894, pp. 254–7. Extract 29: Concluding prayer from Bede's Commentary on Ezra and Nehemiah, original in *Corpus Christianorum*, Latin Series, vol. 119A; Turnhout, Belgium, 1969; English translation by Gerald Bonner.

Picture Acknowledgments

Page 1 (St Luke from MS Lat. Liturg. f.s. St Margaret's gospels), page 14 (Wormwood from the herbal of Ps.–Apuleius and Sextus Placitus, English late 11th century, probably from Bury St Edmunds Abbey), page 18 (Prayer changes the wind. From *Life of St Cuthbert*, University College MS 165 Bede. English. Durham? c. 1150), page 21 (Dropwort, from herbal above), page 23 (Eadberht placed in his tomb, from *Life of St Cuthbert*, above), page 33 (Strawberry, from herbal above), page 35 (from MS Auct. D.2.19, Macregol or Rushworth gospels, Irish (Birr), c. 800), page 41 (Ravens make amends, from *Life of St Cuthbert*, above), page 45 (Bugloss, from herbal above) all reproduced courtesy of the Bodleian Library, Oxford.

Page 2 (The Alfred Jewel) reproduced courtesy of the Ashmolean Museum, University of Oxford.

Pages 2, 3 and 9 (St Matthew's gospel, carpet page, f. 26v (Cott. Nevo.D.IV)), page 4 (St Matthew, opening of the Christmas gospel, f. 29), pages 5 and 6 (St Luke's gospel, detail of the carpet page, f. 138v.), page 7 (St Matthew, detail from initial letter, f. 27), page 15 (St Mark's gospel, carpet page, f. 94), page 17 (detail from St Mark, carpet page), page 25 (St Luke, carpet page, f. 138), page 27 (St Mark, detail from carpet page, f. 94v), page 31 (St John's gospel, carpet page, f. 210v), page 39 (St Luke, detail from initial letter, f. 139) all from the Lindisfarne Gospels by permission of the British Library.